W9-CHZ-244

A creatively painted oil well

Oil

Peter Murray

A⁺

Smart Apple Media

COPYRIGHT

✿ Published by Smart Apple Media

1980 Lookout Drive, North Mankato, MN 56003

Designed by Rita Marshall

Printed in the United States of America

✿ Photographs by Pat Berrett, Horticultural Photography, JLM Visuals (Richard Jacobs, Breck Kent, Mike Reblin), Mo Yung Productions (Peter Parks), Tom Myers

✿ Library of Congress Cataloging-in-Publication Data

Murray, Peter. Oil / by Peter Murray. p. cm. — (From the earth)

Includes index.

✿ ISBN 1-58340-110-5

1. Petroleum—Juvenile literature. [1. Petroleum.] I. Title. II. Series.

TN870.3 .M87 2001   553.2'82—dc21   00-068795

✿ First Edition 9 8 7 6 5 4 3 2 1

Oil

C
O
N
T
E
N
T
S

The Origins of Oil

Hundreds of millions of years ago, the oceans were thick with tiny, floating plants and animals called plankton. As the plankton died, they sank and began to decompose. Thick layers of this decaying, **organic** muck collected at the bottom of the sea. ☀ As the oceans shifted and the earth changed, this muck was covered with sand and silt. Over millions of years, layer after layer formed. The sand and silt hardened to become rock. The organic muck was driven

Oil is formed from decaying organic material

deep into the earth, pressed down by billions of tons of rock.

☀ Very slowly, the heat from the earth's crust and the pressure from the rocks above changed the muck into the slippery black liquid we call oil.

The petroleum that comes from ancient plankton is known as a fossil fuel.

☀ Today's oceans are still filled with plankton. As the plankton organisms die, they sink to the ocean floor and gradually pile up. Hundreds of millions of years from now, each handful of dead plankton might turn into a tiny droplet of oil!

A tiny plankton organism

9

Pipelines to carry oil can be very long

What Is Oil?

The oil that comes out of the ground is called **crude oil**, or petroleum. Crude oil is a thick brown or black mixture of many different hydrocarbons. Hydrocarbons are chemical compounds made of hydrogen and carbon. Examples of hydrocarbons include gasoline, propane, and fuel oil. The motor oil used in car engines is a hydrocarbon. So is the **natural gas** used in gas stoves.

People drill or blast into the ground to find oil

Ancient and Modern Uses of Oil

Oil has been used by humans for more than 4,000 years. Stone-Age humans first discovered seeps—places where underground oil oozed to the surface. The ancient Egyptians used oil from such seeps to grease the axles of their chariots. The Bible says that Noah used pitch, a thick form of oil, to waterproof his ark. American Indians used oil for medicines and war paint. ☀ During the 1800s, oil was used as a lubricant for steam engines and other machinery. But it was not until the invention of the automobile that oil became the

important resource it is today. ☀ Most oil today is used for

fuels to power cars, trucks, ships, planes, and trains. It is also

burned in furnaces to heat homes and businesses. But there

Oil powers most major forms of transportation

are many other uses for oil. Plastics are made from oil. Candles,

insect repellent, aspirin, nail polish, wax, paint, fertilizer,

perfumes, glue, antifreeze, lipstick, and many **The very book you are holding is printed with ink made from oil.**

fabrics are made from petroleum. Even the

laundry detergent we use to clean oil stains

from our clothing is made out of oil! Scientists

have developed more than 500,000 different ways to use

this amazing substance—and new ideas are being generated

every day.

An off-shore rig spilling oil into the sea

Oil and the Future

Oil is a remarkable and useful substance, but it can also be harmful. Burning oil and gas releases hydrocarbons into the air, causing air pollution. Transporting crude oil from wells to refineries also has an impact on the environment. Broken pipelines and spills from oil tankers can harm plants and animals. ☀ Today, humans use more than 70 million barrels of oil every day. Each barrel holds 42 gallons (159 l). To search for new sources of petroleum,

Burning oil releases pollution into the air

wells are drilled miles into the earth's crust. Floating oil rigs probe the ocean depths for oil beneath the bottom of the sea.

☼ Unfortunately, we are using oil much faster than the earth can produce it. Some scientists believe that we will run out of oil within the next 100 years. When the **One of the worst ecological disasters of the last century was the Exxon Valdez oil spill.** oil is gone, we will have to increase our use of other forms of energy, such as solar or nuclear power. But until then, oil will remain one of the world's most valuable resources.

Water contaminated by an oil spill

How Important Is Oil?

H A N D S O N

What You Need

A piece of paper

A pen or pencil

What You Do

Petroleum is an important part of modern life—
but how important is it to *you*? How many different
petroleum products can you see from where you are
sitting right now? Try counting them all. Make a list.
Can you come up with ten? Twenty? A hundred?

Don't forget that everything made out of plastic is a
petroleum product. Anything that uses ink—books,
papers, pens, and printers. Any piece of clothing made
from artificial fibers (nylon, polyester, rayon, etc.—check
the tags!). Anything that uses glue. Anything painted or
dyed. Anything that uses wax—such as candles or pol-
ished wooden furniture.

Oil floating in a water puddle

INFORMATION

Index

Words to Know

crude oil (CROOD OIL)—oil as it comes from the earth; crude oil is a mixture of many different hydrocarbons

natural gas (NAT-chur-ul GAS)—a flammable gas that is found underground, usually with crude oil

organic (or-GAN-ik)—any material that comes from a plant or animal

petroleum (pe-TROLL-ee-um)—another name for crude oil

plankton (PLANK-tun)—microscopic plants and animals that live in the ocean

Read More

Dineen, Jacqueline. *Oil, Gas and Coal.* Austin, Tex.: Raintree Steck-Vaughn, 1995.

Pampe, William R. *Petroleum—How It Is Found and Used.* Hillside, N.J.: Enslow Publishers, 1984.

Twist, Clint. *Facts on Fossil Fuels.* New York: Franklin Watts, 1990.

Internet Sites

Ask-a-Geologist

http://walrus.wr.usgs.gov/docs/ask-a-ge.html/

American Petroleum Institute

http://www.api.org

Air Pollution

http://www.soton.ac.uk/~engenvir/environment/air/air.pollution.html